TOTALLY
TAKE THAT

The Unofficial Guide

by Emily Penn

TOTALLY

TAKE THAT

The Unofficial Guide

by Emily Penn

Written by Emily Penn
Picture Director Francisco Ludovico

Penguin Books
A Penguin Company
Penguin Books Ltd, 80 Strand, London, WC2R 0RL, UK
Penguin Books, Australia Ltd, Camberwell, Victoria, Australia
Penguin Group (NZ), cnr Airborne and Rosedale Roads, Albany,
Auckland 1310, New Zealand

www.penguin.com

ISBN-10: 072325835X
ISBN-13: 9780723258353

Printed in Italy

ORGET . . .

Contents

Introduction

Originally put together by Nigel Martin-Smith as the British answer to New Kids on the Block, Take That went on to become the most successful boy band of all time.

Formed in 1990 in Manchester, Take That dominated the charts for the first half of the '90s, spawning two of the best-selling albums of the decade with *Everything changes* in 1993 and their *Greatest hits* in 1996. They sold a staggering nine million albums and ten million singles during their glittering career.

It was a monumental time for British pop music. Not since the pop bands of the early '80s had the country seen such teen hysteria. There wasn't a man, woman or child in the land who hadn't heard of Take That and most people could name at least two of them – the litmus test of a band's domination.

MACY

Here we look back at the life and times of Take That. The troubled beginnings, the pop supremacy, the departure of one member and the eventual end of an era when the band split up. Now, ten years on, it seems there's a new chapter in the band's story, with a reunion and a new tour – but only with four of the original five members.

Nobody had put on live shows of such glamour and extravagance before. The boys' anthemic pop tunes coupled with the incredible dance routines, ornate costumes and OTT staging set them apart as a pop phenomenon never to be repeated. Though many have tried!

The '90s was a fantastic time for pop and this book is a reminder of the fun, frivolity and flamboyancy of days gone by. It's a time we should never forget.

Before they were famous

ROB

The Facts

Name: Robert Peter Williams
Born: February 13, 1974
Birth place: Stoke-on-Trent
Star sign: Aquarius
Parents: Jan and Pete
Siblings: Sally
School: St Margaret Ward
High School, Stoke

Family Life

After his parents divorced when he was three, Robbie lived with his mother and sister above The Red Lion pub next to the Port Vale football ground. His dad, meanwhile, toured the country's working mens' clubs and holiday resorts as a cabaret entertainer and singer. No prizes for guessing where Rob gets his cheek from then!

Claim to fame

Robbie used to perform at the Theatre Royal in Stoke. He starred in productions of *Chitty Chitty Bang Bang*, *Pickwick*, *Fiddler on the Roof*, *The King and I*, and *Hans Christian Anderson*. But his favourite ever performance was when he played the Artful Dodger in *Oliver Twist*.

First kiss

It was in a boiler room when he was six. The girl's father was in the front room next door and the pair thought they were being very naughty because he could have come in and caught them at any time! Robbie's first Valentine's card was from a girl called Lisa.

14

Previous jobs

Robbie once had a job as a double-glazing salesman. Sadly he wasn't very good at it – he kept telling customers not to buy the company's windows as they were overpriced!

How he got into the band…

Robbie's mum read about an audition for a band in the local paper and arranged for her son to go along.

Did you know…

- Robbie was once punched by a teenage girl after he claimed that Take That were sexier than their American rivals New Kids on the Block.
- Robbie's dyslexic. He's bad with numbers and he gets his b's, d's and nine's round the wrong way.
- He once had a bit part in Brookside.

Robbie was once punched by a teenage girl after he claimed that Take That were sexier than their American rivals New Kids on the Block.

Before they were famous

The Facts

Name: **Gary Barlow**
Born: **January 20, 1971**
Birth place: **Frodsham, Cheshire**
Star sign: **Capricorn**
Parents: **Colin and Marjorie**
Siblings: **Ian**
School: **Frodsham High School**

Family life

His parents' happy marriage always made Gary long for a family of his own. His dad, Colin, was a product manager at United Kingdom Fertilizers and his mum was a science technician at Frodsham High School. Gary says this was an odd experience as whenever he got into trouble the teachers would tell him off and say, 'Watch out Gary or we'll send you to your mum!'

Claim to fame

Gary entered a BBC Pebble Mill competition called *A Song for Christmas* when he was 15 with a ballad he'd written called *Let's pray for Christmas*. He reached the semi-finals of the competition and got to record his song with an orchestra and backing singers, then appeared live on the show singing it.

First kiss

It was with a girl called Melanie Garnett at her seventh birthday party. They ended up being boyfriend and girlfriend for about four years. He reckons they were totally in love and taught each other how to kiss properly.

Gary wrote A million love songs when he was just 15 years old.

Previous jobs

At the age of 11 Gary entered a talent competition at Connah's Quay Labour club, North Wales. He didn't win, but the secretary offered him a job performing cover versions of songs every Saturday night. He was paid £18 per show and stayed for two years – it was a great start for the young singer/songwriter. He then teamed up with a girl called Heather and for the next two years they sang and performed songs by artists like The Carpenters together. When he was 14, Gary landed a job at the Halton British Legion, near Runcorn – playing four gigs over each weekend and clocking off at 2am. He was now earning £140 a night.

How he got into the band…

As part of his Pebble Mill prize, Gary won recording time at Strawberry Studios in Manchester where he met a tea-boy called Mark Owen. Together they formed a band called The Cutest Rush, they sang cover versions and Gary's own compositions. It was as part of this duo that Gary first went to see Nigel Martin-Smith.

Did you know…

- Gary used to play the organ for Ken Dodd.
- Gary wrote *A million love songs* and *It only takes a minute* when he was just 15 years old.
- His old music teacher, Mrs Born, always used to tell him off for drumming on his desk with a ruler. She told him he wouldn't ever earn a living from music.
- Gary left school with six O levels.

Before they were famous

The Facts

Name: Jason Thomas Orange
Born: July 10, 1970
Birth place: Manchester
Star sign: Cancer
Parents: Tony and Jenny
Siblings: Simon, Dominic, Justin (his twin),
Samuel, Oliver and half-sisters Emma and Amy,
step-brother Simon and step-sister Sarah
School: South Manchester High School

Family life

Jason's parents divorced when he was young –
he says it was the saddest thing that ever
happened to him. His mum raised him and his
five brothers on her own. He would see his dad
from time to time, but he said that it wasn't a
real father and son relationship; they would just
be polite to each other, more like strangers. His
mum had a part-time job in a doctor's surgery.

School

Jason was quite shy at school and never used to
talk or join in discussions in class.

First kiss

It was with a girl called Karen when he was
12. She was his friend Neil's sister and he was
so desperate to get his first snog out of the way
that he just grabbed her one day when they were
in his garden. Unfortunately, she had her dog
with her who didn't like what he was doing and
jumped up and pawed him. Poor Jason ran off.
He says it was a pretty atrocious experience!

Jason got a job as a painter/decorator with a company called Direct Works.

How he got into the band…

If it wasn't for a friend's girlfriend Jason might never have made it into Take That. She realized what a fabulous dancer he was and wrote to *The Hitman and Her*, a music show presented by Pete Waterman and Michaela Strachan, telling them all about Jason. He loved to break-dance and had joined a crew called Street Machine who he used to dance with in Manchester's clubs. *The Hitman and Her* asked Jason to audition for the show – he became a regular! It was there he met Howard Donald who was in a rival act. They formed their own crew called Street Beat and came to the attention of Nigel Martin-Smith.

Previous jobs

Jason and Justin joined a Youth Training Scheme and through that, Jason got a job as a painter/decorator with a company called Direct Works. Despite his later fame, Jason always kept in touch with his old work mate Ray Smith.

Did you know…

- Jason is a vegetarian. He initially gave up meat altogether for both health and animal cruelty reasons but he lost so much weight that he became ill. For a little while he had to start eating a bit of chicken and fish again to build himself back up.

- Jason was never really bothered about being in a pop group – he just wanted to be a good dancer!

Before they were famous

The Facts

Name: **Mark Anthony Patrick Owen**
Born: **January 27, 1972**
Birth place: **Oldham, Greater Manchester**
Star sign: **Aquarius**
Parents: **Keith and Mary**
Siblings: **Daniel and Tracy**
School: **St Augustine's Catholic School**

Family life

Mark's family lived in a small council house that looked like it was out of the cobbled streets of Coronation Street. He shared a room with his brother Daniel. His dad, Keith, used to be a decorator and then got a job in a police station. His mum, Mary, was a supervisor at a bakery in Oldham.

First kiss

Mark's first crush was on his babysitter Jackie. But his first kiss was when he was nine and was playing Truth or Dare with his friends. Her name was Michelle. Mark didn't actually have a proper girlfriend until he was 13.

School

Mark starred in a lot of the school plays but his favourite one was when he played Jesus. His favourite teacher was Mrs Proctor who taught art.

MARK

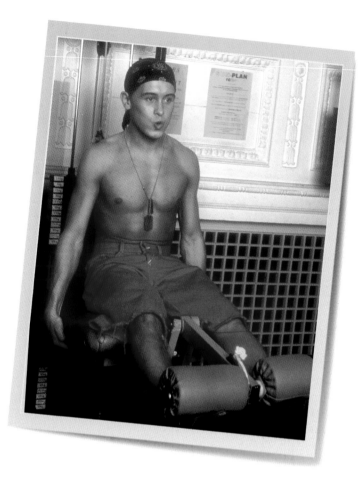

His Saturday job, as a tea-boy at Strawberry Studios, was where he met Gary.

Previous jobs

His first job was as a shop assistant in a clothes boutique called Zutti's before he went on to work at the local Barclays Bank. Then, to earn extra money he took a Saturday job at Strawberry Studios as a tea-boy.

Other achievements

Mark was a very good footballer and even had trials with Huddersfield Town, Manchester United and Rochdale football clubs, but he damaged his groin and had to give it up.

How he got into the band…

His Saturday job, at Strawberry Studios, was where he met Gary, and the rest, as they say, is history…

Did you know…

- **Mark's scared of wasps. He had a bad reaction once when he was stung on the ear while on holiday in Majorca and freaks out now every time one flies near him!**
- **Mark had a pet iguana called Nirvana.**
- **According to his teachers, Mark showed no interest in music at school, he was too busy running around the football pitch.**

Before they were famous

The Facts

Name: Howard Paul Donald
Born: April 28, 1968
Birth place: Manchester
Star sign: Taurus
Parents: Keith and Kathleen
Siblings: Michael, Colin, Glenn and Samantha
School: Little Moss High School for Boys

Family life

Howard's parents divorced when he was eight although he stayed close to his dad. He and his brothers and sister lived with his mum, Kathleen, and her new husband, Mike. Kathleen was a secretary at an infants' school and his dad, Keith, used to be a Latin-American dance teacher – so we know where Howard got his moves from!

First kiss

Howard had his first girlfriend when he was 11 and he had his first kiss with her. She never knew that at the time he thought he was in love. Sweet!

Previous jobs

After school, Howard got an apprenticeship at Knibbs in Manchester, a company that specialized in spraying cars. After that he got his first job at Wimpole Garages, restoring cars. He worked there for two years. But it was the break-dancing he did in his spare time with the RDS Royal crew that he really loved.

Earliest memory

Playing Cowboys and Indians in his friend's back garden. Howard threw his gun at another boy and it whacked him on the head. The boy's head was cut badly and there was blood everywhere. Howard ran home and hid in the bathroom until the boy's parents turned up. He was terrified, but his mum sorted it out!

How he got into the band…

Just like Jason, Howard was a massive break-dancer. As we know it was fated that they should meet on the set of *The Hitman and Her!*

Did you know…

- Howard was a bit of a tearaway at school and once bunked off for a whole five weeks! But he didn't get off scott free, when he was eventually found out, he got the cane!
- He also had a really big crush on one of his teachers and had his heart broken because she never noticed him…

Howard got an apprenticeship at Knibbs in Manchester, a company that specialized in spraying cars.

History in the making

FIRST IMPRE

Nigel Martin-Smith's dream of a British version of New Kids On The Block began with Jason and Howard. The boys had taken their break-dancing act, Street Beat, into him and he was very impressed. But it wasn't until he met Mark and Gary, when they were Cutest Rush, that he saw the potential. Here were four strong, determined individuals who had something for everyone...

…but they were just missing one vital ingredient! The cheeky joker.

Nigel put an advert in a local Manchester paper for a fifth member. One young Robert Peter Williams applied. Robbie sang a song from Joseph and the Amazing Technicolour Dreamcoat for his audition.

What did they think?

- Universally they all thought that Mark was really cute.
- Mark thought that Jason was an amazing dancer. He tried to have a go too, but his attempts just brought howls of laughter from the rest of the lads.
- Jason remembered Gary as being really confident and nice.

- Legend has it that Robbie thought they were an odd bunch of lads and didn't really see how they would gel as a unit.
- Howard found Gary a little bit quiet at first.
- Not surprisingly, Gary thought Jason and Howard were amazing dancers and was pretty intimidated by how good they were! He was probably worried about the moves that he would have to perform later!

In the **beginning...**

LEATHER

It was tough. And it wasn't just because of the leather-studded jockstraps they used to wear! It was the days of the pretty pop of Kylie and Jason and the techno beats of 2Unlimited. The UK wasn't ready for five hip-swinging, pelvic-thrusting, Northern lads with big gobs and even bigger ideas. Not that that was going to stop them!

Shortly after the band was formed, they had their first gig at a club called Flicks in Huddersfield. Only 30 people showed up but the boys were delighted anyway – they'd done it, they'd got on stage and performed. They only got £20 each, but it was enough for a KFC on the way home. They were happy.

The first year was spent touring every nightclub in the country – they weren't the classiest of joints, but that only added to the fun. Soon their name was getting known and their first TV appearance followed on a satellite show called *Cool Cube*. Next came an even bigger gig – they were booked for *The Hitman and Her*.

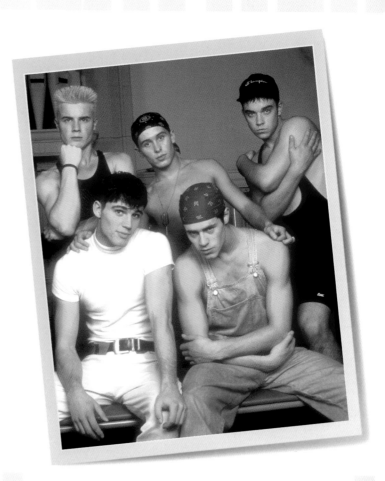

In the meantime…

Nigel had visited every record company in the land, but no one was biting. They decided to go it alone. Their first single, *Do what u like*, was released on Nigel's own label, Dance UK, in July 1991. It only reached No. 82, but it got them noticed. Not least because the video revolved around the five of them having jelly rubbed into their naked bodies!

STUDDED
JOCK STRAPS

In the beginning...

Take That were signed by RCA Records in September 1991 and the boys thought that they'd finally made it. After they signed the deal they were flown to London. They were bowled over by the flashy limousine that was waiting at the airport. They just couldn't believe that it was there for them and that they were going to be pop stars!

Their second single, *Promises*, was released in November 1991 and went in at No. 38. The boys were staying at the Regency Hotel in London when they heard. They were so chuffed that Howard's bed broke because they were bouncing up and down on it so much. But by the next week it had dropped down to No. 40.

The decision was made to get another record out as soon as possible. *Once you've tasted love* was released in January 1992. It was a disaster, charting at No. 47. The boys were upset but determined not to give up. But what they didn't know was that RCA was in crisis talks over what had turned out to be an embarrassing fiasco. If it hadn't been for their loyal A&R man Nick Raymond sticking his neck out for them, they would have been history.

It was back to the drawing board and the ground-breaking decision was made to send the boys on a tour of schools up and down the country. The band played three schools a day and reached thousands of young girls who were just waiting for a group they could finally get excited about. Surely the time was right?

It only takes **a minute**

PELVIC

It was decided that the band should release a cover version and Nigel chose the old disco song, *It only takes a minute* by Tavares. Not everyone was keen.

Howard said that when he first heard it in the office he didn't really like it. But the mix they did proved to be pretty catchy and irresistible!

Take That were in a restaurant in Fulham called *La Reserve* when the first chart position came in. It was No. 15. They had made the Top 20 and finally cracked it. There were even fans outside the restaurant crying with joy, but the best was yet to come.

[**It only takes a minute**
Released May 1992
Highest chart position 7]

As the record steadily climbed, one of their biggest dreams was about to be realized... an appearance on *Top of the Pops*. But it wasn't to be as glamorous as they expected. Gary didn't think that pop music was very fashionable when Take That started out. Inevitably, as with most new bands, there was a backlash with the boys being accused of having no talent. Apparently the Top of the Pops crew had a wager between themselves on whether they could actually sing at all!

THRUSTING

Fortunately, someone decided that the leather had had its day and these outfits were consigned to the dustbin. For the video, the boys wore vests, tracksuit bottoms and trainers. They shot the video in the same boxing gym where the Krays trained.

Inevitably there was a backlash . . .

When it was time to devise the dance routine, Jason and Howard were both in bad moods and couldn't really be bothered. They choreographed it separately at Howard's house. They each came up with their own bits and pieces, which they then just mixed all together in a few hours. Amazingly it worked!

Take That **and Party**

AUGUST

Take That and Party was the band's first album and it was released in August 1992. It reached No. 2 in the chart.

Track listing

I found heaven
Once you've tasted love
It only takes a minute
A million love songs
Satisfied
I can make it
Do what u like
Promises
Why can't I wake up with you
Never want to let you go
Give good feeling
Could it be magic
Take That and party

I found heaven
Released August 1992
Highest chart position 15

The next single release, *I found heaven*, was one of the boys' least favourites – and incidentally one of the few not written by Gary. But it did introduce a baby-faced Robbie to the nation as he shared lead vocal duties with Gary.

To get inspiration for the routine, Jason and Howard watched a few old Drifters and Four Tops videos to try and inject a bit of soul into it.

Apparently Rob and Gary had their own secret lyrics which they sometimes used to sing to this one. And they were extremely rude!

It was unreservedly sloppy and slushy, but it also brought Take That to the attention of a whole new audience – housewives, mums and grannies.

1992

It was going well, but there was still a feeling of unease as to whether the band would ever be as big as all involved had hoped. And because of this, it was decided to keep pumping the songs out with *A million love songs* being released barely a month after *Heaven*.

A million love songs
Released September 1992
Highest chart position 7

Originally the video was supposed to have been the band in cartoon form, but when they painted over the footage it looked dreadful. So the idea was scrapped and the finished video became the rough black and white footage first shot.

The big time

Who would ever have thought that crooner Barry Manilow could be cool?! But that's what happened when TT's version of this old classic stormed up the charts to the No. 3 slot! Robbie took lead vocals on his own for the very first time, even impressing old Barry by all accounts. Shortly after the single was released, Manilow played at the Apollo Theatre in Manchester and had a young boy come out and sing and dance to it just like Robbie!

As the Take That convoy started gaining pace, the decision was made to release a seventh single from the band's debut album. Cynics talked of milking the fans, but most accepted that as it had been a slow start, it made sense to now capitalise on their success and keep it rolling.

Why can't I wake up with you
Released February 1993
Highest chart position 2

The song gave them their highest chart position to date as its sultry, more mature air obviously broadened their fanbase even further.

Could it be magic
Released December 1992
Highest chart position 3

The band got their first taste of real luxury when they filmed this video as they got to stay in the beautiful French chateau where the video was filmed. But they still weren't being treated as stars – Nigel was running round telling them not to break anything as they'd have to pay for it and they couldn't afford anything in there!

The elusive No. 1

The band had never really stopped touring, but the Take That and Party arena tour was the first of their really spectacular stage shows.

Could it be magic
Best British Single
BRIT AWARD 1993

With numerous costume changes and the blisteringly hot dance routines, the band set the live benchmark for every future generation of pop band. But it was the extras that really set them apart. From Robbie's funky raps to Howard's strange denim skirts and headscarves, everything about their live performances was designed to excite. And it was never about one getting more glory than the others. Everyone knew Gary couldn't dance and he stood back and watched admiringly as the others did their thing. Jason was never the strongest singer, but he still got his moment when he finished off the Motown medley they used to perform with his own unique version of *I feel good* by James Brown.

Take That scooped an unprecedented seven awards at that year's Smash Hits ceremony.

Everybody was talking about these five Northern lads and even though record sales weren't as phenomenal as had been expected, by the time *A million love songs* charted, Take That were the absolute darlings of the teen world. Take That scooped an unprecedented seven awards at that year's Smash Hits ceremony.

And it wasn't just the band's loyal fans that were going crazy for them – the hysteria was spreading to the industry too. In the same year, Take That won a Brit Award for Best British single for *Could it be magic*.

Everything was there. The shows, the videos, the press attention. Everything, well almost everything. They still hadn't managed that elusive No. 1…

Prayers are answered

Gary knew the moment they finished recording this song that they had something special. There was a catchy melody and a memorable chorus. Everyone felt that all the vital elements had come together in this song to give them that all-important breakthrough.

CHART

The record company were obviously fairly confident too as it was the first time that the band were taken some-where really exotic to film the video. They went to Acapulco.

But despite the much larger budget and more glamorous location, things still didn't go quite to plan… For the final scene in the video they didn't have enough gospel singers to fill the line-up, so various members of the crew were drafted in. One of the band's security guards was even recruited to sing and sway along. A lot of these extras had no idea of the lyrics and can be seen miming to nothing in particular!

Pray
Released July 1993
Highest chart position 1

The band was travelling from home to a place in Wales for rehearsal when they heard that *Pray* had made it to No. 1. For many years Mark had been taping the top 40 countdown each week. He would replay this particular countdown time and time again, reliving this magical moment!

Even though this song was to come off the next album, the group still managed to get it into their Take That and Party tour and it became one of their favourite songs to perform live. Sometimes they would come out dressed head to toe in black cloaks like monks, while other times they would be all in white, like angels.

…things still didn't go quite to plan.

Take That at the top!

Fame

For Robbie it was the loss of his privacy that he found hardest to cope with. He found it difficult to be public property.

He has even had people follow him into the loo to ask for an autograph while he was peeing. Someone once even asked to have their picture taken with him in there.

Being normal

No amount of fame would ever put him off going to seen his beloved Port Vale play though. He would arrive just before kick off then go into the sponsor's box afterwards for a few drinks until most of the crowds had left.

Image

Robbie has always had problems with his weight and at the peak of Take That's fame he put himself on a strict diet so that he would be in tip top shape for the tours. He tried to avoid all dairy produce and white bread and would eat lots of tuna and chicken. When he was at home he would sometimes eat a whole chicken in a day with just a bit of salt on the side.

...sometimes he would eat a whole chicken in a day...

Friends

His best mate throughout everything has been Jonathan Wilkes. The pair met at school and despite everything have remained very close friends. In fact Robbie has often accredited him with being his only real friend.

Robbie would also worry about fame changing him and would constantly be asking people if he had become big-headed yet.

The joker

Robbie used to rely on his own sense of humour for entertainment. He was notorious for creating a fictitious life for himself just to keep himself occupied during interviews. When he used to read his interviews back he would hate it if he felt he hadn't been funny enough.

Robbie thinks he missed out on a lot of the normal stuff, like hanging out with mates because he got into the band so young. He lost touch with all his school friends and then once he got famous it was too late to make new ones. When he did get on well with someone Robbie was always worried incase they liked him because of what he was rather than who he was.

Take That **at the top!**

Travel

Robbie's favourite countries when he was on tour were Holland and Japan. Once while in Amsterdam the band visited a bar called *The Bulldog* which had karaoke. Robbie got up and did a version of *Mack the Knife*. It seemed that no one recognized him as a pop star, but he still managed to get a standing ovation from the crowd.

Another time when they were in Hong Kong, the guys decided to try lobster and it led to one of Robbie's favourite moments. The waiter had carried a live lobster up to the table for them to inspect, but Gary was somehow unaware of its approach. When he turn round he jumped out of his seat when he eyeballed the huge crustacean!

Robbie extra – Read all about it!

Rumour has it that the Robster used to take his dirty washing back to his mum's after a tour!

Robbie's confirmation name is Maximillian.

The young Robbie originally wanted to be an actor not a pop star. Michael Caine is one of his all-time favourite actors.

Robbie's comedian dad, Pete Conway, once won the talent show New Faces.

Robbie is the tallest member of Take That at 6′ 1″.

Robbie's nickname was 'Baby'.

Robbie is a keen rollerblader.

Take That **at the top!**

Image

After seeing his *Spitting Image* puppet on TV, Gary was determined to lose some weight and drafted the band's resident Mr Motivator, Jason, in to help him! He also said that being constantly surrounded by four muscly, good-looking blokes made him feel incredibly paranoid.

Party animal

After a gig, when most pop stars are trashing their hotel rooms, Gary would dash back to his room and get stuck into the latest edition of *Homes and Interiors* magazine.

Travel

Gary was always amazed by how quiet and polite the Japanese fans were. After one show as the band returned to their dressing room there were about 30 girls screaming outside for them. One of their security guards shouted, 'Shut-up!' and they all did! Instant silence.

Fans

He reckoned that the band's fanbase was so loyal that at one time if they put a record out with the boys burping on it, it would probably have become a hit.

Fame

Gary said that for him fame was everything he thought it would be and more. The fact that he could sit back at home and know that people all over the world might be listening to his music made him really happy.

Love life

Gary says that he's never been that good with the ladies. He wrote A *million love songs* about the fact that he's written love song after love song yet he could never say 'I love you'.

. . . if they put a record out with the boys burping on it, it would probably have become a hit.

Take That **at the top!**

Famous fans

One of Gary's proudest moments was when he first met Elton John. Elton told him that he had a talent and if he wanted to he could make a career out of songwriting for life. Gary said he hadn't thought about it like that before and from that day his life changed. He knew that whatever happened with Take That as a band, he would be able to earn a living from music.

Gary extra – Read all about it!

Gary is a bit of an horologist on the side! He spends many an hour studying time with his collection of clocks!

Rumour has it that Gary, in moments of weakness, loved to tuck into a tub of Haagen Dazs ice cream!

Whilst the other boys in the band regularly had cuddly toys thrown at them, it is said that Gary's fans used to send him copies of interior design magazines! Very rock and roll Mr Barlow!

Gary loves living in the countryside. He has a recording studio at home so he doesn't even have to travel to work!

Gary might want to think about becoming a policeman!!

Gary's mum thought that the world of pop wasn't very stable and she once suggested that Gary might want to think about becoming a policeman!!

Gary was always sensitive to the fact that he earned more money than the rest of the band from his songwriting royalties.

Take That **at the top!**

Fame

Jason never dreamed that the band would be as big as it was and he really thought that he didn't deserve it. He would feel guilty that there were more talented people than him struggling to make it. Jason put his success down to luck – being in the right place at the right time!

The early days

Jason actually considered leaving the band early on in his career because he didn't think he would be able to take the pressure of being a teen idol. He was planning on going back to painting and decorating.

The future

At the height of their success, Jason was already planning ahead and had designs on becoming a manager, but not of a pop band. For him it would have to have been a rock or a grunge group.

Religion

Jason was always the most spiritual out of the group and would often have long discussions about Christianity and Buddhism. He was also the loner and after tours would take himself off on holiday alone, just with a book for company, usually to his favourite destination, Mauritius.

Royalty

Jason is actually a direct descendant of King William of Orange who reigned Britain in the 17th century, and was also a member of the Dutch royal family.

The leader

Jason always said that it was good to have Gary in the group when things were strained as he was the calming factor and would always make the right decisions.

Jason was always the most spiritual out of the group and would often have long discussions about Christianity and Buddhism.

Take That **at the top!**

Diet

Jason had a phobia of filling up his body with unhealthy foods and because of that would eat no fat, no dairy products, no artificial sugars and no caffeine. In fact the only naughty thing he ever did treat himself to was his beloved curries – the hotter the better!

Improving himself

Along with reading numerous self-help books, Jason also took up the guitar and taught himself to play. He was very disciplined with himself and would practice faithfully each day.

Nightmares

Jason often used to have dreams about beating the rest of the band up, but he was philosophical about it. He wouldn't let these disturbing images worry him. He was secure in the fact they were just nightmares and nothing related to real life.

Jason often used to have dreams about beating the rest of the band up.

Jason extra – Read all about it!

When Jason first met Nigel Martin-Smith at *The Hitman and Her* set, Jason didn't show much interest in being in a band – he was happy to be a dancer.

Jason is a dancing perfectionist – he would practise for hours and made sure the rest of the band did too.

Jason is only 20 minutes older than his twin brother, Justin.

At school, Jason wasn't very academic. But he's made up for it since – he was the bookworm of Take That!

Interestingly, Jason metamorphosed from the shy one at school, to an out-and-out exhibitionist in Take That!

Jason is not a good flyer – he would usually sit at the front of the plane nervously.

Jason used to wear a woolly hat and a pair of glasses as a disguise when he went shopping.

He is happy to spend time on his own. He often goes out for a curry with just a book for company.

Take That **at the top!**

The worrier

Even at the height of the band's success, Mark worried about everything. He would worry about Jason's injuries, or the girls outside the hotel getting cold or if the fans were getting enough value for money. Everything.

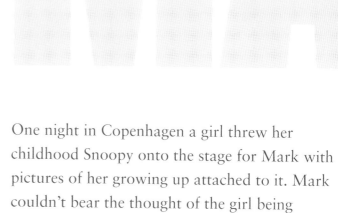

One night in Copenhagen a girl threw her childhood Snoopy onto the stage for Mark with pictures of her growing up attached to it. Mark couldn't bear the thought of the girl being separated from her toy, so the next day wrote her a lovely letter and sent it back.

The cute one

Mark was always the most popular in the band. If ever there was an award for 'Most Fanciable' or 'Biggest Heart-throb' Mark would win it, but it never went to his head.

Travel

Mark's favourite country was America and he said that one of his most memorable moments was when they were recognized in New York. They were sitting on a park bench being interviewed by Simon Bates when a girl walked up and said, 'Hello lads, what are you doing here?'

Jason's mum, Mary, was wary of her son joining Take That. He'd only just got a job in a bank and being a popstar seemed to be miles from reality. But Nigel managed to persuade her that the band would succeed.

RK

Practice makes perfect!

Mark decided to have some singing lessons to help with the strength of his voice, so he bought himself some karaoke tapes and used to sit in his bedroom singing alone on his mic.

Mark was always the most popular in the band. If ever there was an award for 'Most fanciable' or 'Biggest Heart-throb' Mark would win it.

Keeping fit

While on tour Mark liked to try to keep fit. He and Rob used to do weights together, but one day Mark decided to go for a run. The path that he followed was pretty long and eventually led him onto some major road – Mark thought he was on a motorway! He ran so far that for the next few days he was hobbling around with stiff calf muscles!

Take That at the top!

Chatterbox

Mark was renowned for talking to himself! He would often be spotted just wandering around jabbering aimlessly away to no one in particular. He used to do it to journalists too. When he was being interviewed he would often grab the tape recorder and wander off chatting away into it. Goodness knows what rubbish they'd find on there when they got home!

Vegetarians

After long conversations with Jason about meat, Mark eventually gave it up for good and has always said that he's never, ever missed it.

A royal affair

When the band had tea with Princess Diana after the Concert of Hope on World Aids Day, Mark knew it was an opportunity he couldn't miss as he'd always said that if he ever met her, he would ask her out. So he did. He asked her if she was free on Sunday and fancied going out. She politely smiled and said that she was sorry, but she was busy, but thanked him for asking.

[He asked Princess Diana if she was free on Sunday and fancied going out.]

RK

Mark extra – Read all about it!

Mark's first musical idol was Elvis – he does a mean impression of the King!

Mark was worried that his mum would think that the stage show for the band's summer tour in 1993 was too raunchy! For their last song, *It only takes a minute*, the boys dropped their trousers! Instead of bare bottoms, their underpants spelled out Take That!

Take That **at the top!**

Fame

Howard has remained adamant that fame never changed him. He believed that it actually changed the attitude of the people around him. He thought they assumed that he was pretentious and big-headed, but he wanted everyone to know that if they took the time to speak to him, they'd realise that he was just the same old Howard as before.

Like Robbie, Howard missed his privacy when the band eventually struck the big time. Naturally reserved, he found the limelight sometimes too much to handle.

Howard was adamant that fame never changed him. He believed that it actually changed the attitude of the people around him.

Groupies

Ever the gentleman, Howard didn't approve of exploiting his position as a pop star with groupies. He just didn't see himself as the "love 'em and leave 'em" type.

Travel

Howard really liked Japan. One time when they were touring there it was raining heavily – Howard reminisced fondly of Manchester!

Regrets

As the band were becoming more and more successful, the boys didn't get the chance to see as much of their families as they would have liked. Howard always regrets that he didn't manage to see much of his grandfather who then passed away shortly afterwards. Howard often thinks of the things he should have said to him.

Take That at the top!

The thinker

Howard can't help his mind going off on strange trains of thought. For example, he was once on stage and was looking out into the crowd wondering if any of the girls in the audience had lost their parents and it made him really sad. He always empathized with his fellow band members when things were tough. Howard was known to be a good listener and a great shoulder to cry on.

HOW

Hobbies

Howard treated himself to a new keyboard and mixing desk and would often spend any spare time he had at home on his own just tinkering around on it.

Howard extra – Read all about it!

Howard's nickname was Centrefold – no prizes for guessing why! Just look at that broad chest!!!

Howard once appeared on *Come Dancing!* He wasn't performing a waltz or tango but a break-dancing version of *Seven Brides for Seven Brothers!*

Howard wasn't the most focussed of students when it came to academia – he left school with no qualifications!

Howard has a thing about chest hairs! He pulls them out if he spots one!

The early gigs that Howard and Jason did as Street Beat earned them £25 a night.

Relight my fire

The boys already loved this Dan Hartman track as they used to dance to it in the clubs when they were young. They were nervous that they'd never be able to do a version that came close. But as soon as they discovered that Lulu was going to be singing on it with them, they knew that it was all going to be alright.

Jason was particularly pleased that he'd be singing with Lulu. 'My elder brother, Simon fancies her,' he said at the time, 'and when I told him she was on our track he was dead jealous.'

Mark has slightly more down to earth memories of working with the lady. 'I remember she turned up with a flask of tea,' he said.

H LULU

Relight my fire
Released September 1993
Highest chart position 1

The video was shot in London's trendy Ministry of Sound nightclub and was one of their weirdest, filled with transvestites, monsters and Mark's favourite, 'the red balloon man'. Mark also got into trouble with the record company for the 'Junkie's Baddy Powder' t-shirt he wore. They felt he was setting a bad example.

Jason was very proud of the *Relight* routine, 'It's a fast routine, funked up, man, it's bang on.' It was also about this time that other boy bands started to appear, which Jason was very aware of… 'No disrespect to anybody else, but we had to show them who was the best.'

When the band performed *Relight my fire* at Euro Disney, they shared the stage with a group of Disney characters. Robbie had somehow discovered that Mickey Mouse was in fact a woman! He and the boys kept pinching her bottom. Suffice it to say, Mickey was not a happy mouse!

Robbie was originally meant to be singing lead vocal, but when they went into the studio, it didn't actually suit his voice, so it was handed back to Gary.

61

The second album
TAKE THAT &

Track Listing

Everything changes
Pray
Wasting my time
Relight my fire
Love ain't here anymore
If this is love
Whatever you do to me
Meaning of love
Why can't I wake up with you
You are the one
Another crack in my heart
Broken your heart
Babe

While the band didn't give many interviews anymore, they still showed their gratitude to the press and everyone they worked with during those days by throwing some of the best parties the pop world had ever seen.

For this tour, they took some of their favourite journalists to Munich to see the show before it came to the UK. After an amazing concert, the boys hosted a party at a cool basement club in the centre of town. At the party guests were given a menu where every song on the album was a different cocktail – so of course you had to try them all at least once! Robbie kept being given a Relight – whether he asked for it or not! Just before everyone left the club the whole band got on the bar and did a dance routine. Quite a sight! The party continued at the hotel with Robbie as DJ and Mark leading the dancing till the wee hours.

Another truly memorable night, was when the boys were presented with the key to their city – Manchester. The mayoress hosted a large party at the town hall, which had been turned into a casino for the night! There were even Take That chips on the card tables! Later in the evening one of the rooms was turned into a nightclub – Howard got on the decks and rocked the crowd – a taste of things to come perhaps…

Then a very lucky few were invited to Earl's Court where the band were rehearsing their most impressive tour to date – they even had a suspended walkway.

PARTY
PARTY

After a slap-up meal and chat with the boys, they performed their entire show for a handful of people in an empty arena.

No one will ever forget walking underneath the walkway as the boys did their stuff above. The only slight hitch to the proceedings was when Mark performed *Babe* for the very first time with the video played on a huge screen. He was supposed to walk through just as his video figure came forward on screen... The only problem was, someone had forgotten the video – so he had to step through a blank screen! But everyone got the idea.

Babe

TAKE THAT &

Mark and Jason worked on *Babe* for six months in order to get it just right. Jason practised like mad on the guitar with Mark warbling away alongside him.

Babe
Released December 1993
Highest chart position 1

Because the song was such a beautiful ballad, it was decided that it had to be sung very softly which was why Mark was chosen. All the boys thought Mark did a brilliant job. Even Mark was surprised when he first heard it. 'Does my voice really sound like that?' he asked at the time.

Apparently Gary does a mean country and western version of this song.

Babe almost stayed at the top to become the Christmas No. 1, but unfortunately it was knocked off by... Mr Blobby!

PARTY PARTY

It had to be sung very softly which was why Mark was chosen.

The video was filmed near Canary Wharf in London, in a disused factory. Everyone really enjoyed filming it as they got to act for the first time. Robbie and Mark especially enjoyed revisiting their dramatic roots!

After the shoot the boys all agreed that their favourite shot was of Howard on his bike in his funny old-fashioned clothes.

Howard remembers the first time they all saw the finished version of the video. They had just played live at Wembley and they all dashed back to their tour coach to watch it. He reckons there was more than one pair of misty eyes by the end, although he thinks the reason Gary had tears in his eyes because he couldn't stop laughing at him on that bike! 'He kept having to rewind it to have a good laugh,' he grumbled at the time.

Everything changes
FOURTH No. 1

Half-way through writing the *Everything changes* album Gary realized that Robbie didn't have lead vocals on any of the songs. He explained the situation to the guys he was working with and, hey presto, *Everything changes*, the single, was born.

Everyone's highlight from the video shoot was the cute little boy dancing around with them. He was a great little dancer with lots of funky moves. And at only around seven years old, he out-danced the rest of the band!

It was about this time that Jason grew his hair for the first time. It was a bit shaggy and a bit grungy but people seemed to like it, so he kept it.

When they were recording the video, Jason said that he used to love watching the expressions on Robbie's face when he had to sing the first line 'Forever more…', as it was so high for him.

When they were coming up with the routine for the song, there was a kind of skipping move they did that didn't actually make it into the final sequence, but Gary loved it. He used to do it all the time. 'I've got this one!' he'd yell, and then skip off into the distance!

[Everything changes
Released March 1994
Highest chart position 1]

Love ain't here anymore

THE FIFTH

This was the fifth single released from the *Everything changes* album and some thought it was one too many, especially as they wanted their run of Number one's to continue… But, as it turned out, it probably wouldn't have made much of a difference what they released as Wet Wet Wet hogged the top of the charts all summer with *Love is all around*.

[
Love ain't here anymore
Released June 1994
Highest chart position 3
]

SINGLE

They were after
an arty and brooding
look, but in reality it
came over as a bit,
well, boring.

The video for *Love ain't here* is probably the one least liked by the whole band. It was originally meant to be a bit like Madonna's *Rain* video, but for some reason it didn't quite work. They were after an arty and brooding look, but in reality it came over as a bit, well, boring.

There was never a really cohesive stage look for this song, and as a result it always used to end up being sandwiched into the middle of the live set. More often than not the boys were usually still in their lumberjack shirts and knee length boots when they performed it!

Mark's favourite memory of *Love ain't here anymore* is that someone told him he looked like Suede's Brett Anderson on the single sleeve, which he was very pleased about.

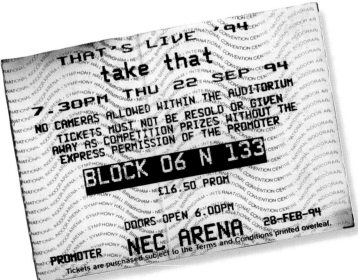

Sure

A SURE-FIR

It was straight back to the top with *Sure*, the first single from the *Nobody else* album. It was also a different sound for the band. There was a move away from the pretty pop of previous hits. Now the sound was harder, funkier and edgier.

Gary told Mark and Robbie to go away and write a middle eight for *Sure* and within 30 minutes the two of them returned with the 'holdin', squeezin', touchin' bit. Unfortunately on the first day of recording, Mark left his all-important lyrics at home and they had to start from scratch trying to remember what they were!

> There was a move away from the pretty pop of previous hits, now the sound was harder, funkier and edgier.

The first time Gary played the song to the rest of the band was round an old piano in a bar in Belgium. They all liked it straight away.

Both Howard and Jason really liked the song and wanted the dance routine to be absolutely perfect. They wanted the moves to mirror the new sound. Unfortunately, when they came to perform it for the first time for Nigel, Mark got stung by a wasp and ran off. From that point on they all went to pieces. Nigel wasn't that impressed by the routine after all.

E HIT

[
Sure
Released October 1994
Highest chart position 1
]

The band wanted to try out their hands at acting for this video. They loved the fact that they had lines to deliver, but they couldn't believe the amount of work that went into creating those few scenes.

Howard had a bit of trouble with his eyebrow that day. He'd just had it pierced and it was just starting to swell up, so he had to rely on the kindness of the make-up lady to keep cleaning it for him every two minutes to try to keep the puffiness at bay.

Back for good

Back for good is probably Take That's most well known and critically acclaimed song. This song was the one that really crossed borders for them, everyone from little kids in the playground to your 90-year-old granny knew all the words. It was the first of their tracks to be successful in America, plus of course, Gary won an Ivor Novello Award for it.

Gary wrote it in about 15 minutes. He's always said that the songs he wrote the fastest were the best.

Back for good
Released March 1995
Highest chart position 1

Originally Mark was supposed to sing lead on this track, but when Gary was messing around in the studio singing the 'Back for good' line over and over, the producer heard him and insisted that he have a go at the whole song because it sounded great. So Mark was given *The day after tomorrow* to sing instead, which was a song that really complimented his sweet voice.

The video was one of their most striking, although funnily enough probably one of their simplest. Even though the boys all love the finished product, they don't have fond memories of the actual filming...

Howard was extremely pleased that it was him who got to drive the cool vintage American car.

It was shot at Pinewood Studios on a freezing cold day and they were being blasted by rain machines. Apparently Robbie had the hardest time as he'd just shaved all his hair off. The rain pelting his bald head was incredibly painful.

With the song reaching No. 7 in the US Billboard charts, the band got to do a proper promotional tour there for the very first time. They appeared on the *David Letterman Show* as well as performing outside the Rockefeller Centre in New York for a TV show – where it rained on cue. But their highlight was when they performed it live on a big radio show with just Jason on guitar and the four vocalists. Everyone who heard it thought it was absolutely beautiful.

Everyone who heard it thought it was absolutely beautiful.

Nobody else

Have you ever wondered what all that junk was surrounding the Take That dolls on the cover of the *Nobody Else* album? Well, it's actually not junk at all, it is in fact some of the boys' very own most treasured items. Take out your old vinyl and have a closer look.

Dalek toothbrush holder
This was Gary's from when he was a child. He used to love Dr Who.

The book
It's called the *The Art of Wisdom* and Mark was heavily into it at the time of the shoot. It's full of philosophical thoughts and sayings.

The pouch
It was Robbie's when he was very young, but he didn't know what was in it and he wouldn't look. The others had a feel and thought it was either a baby tooth or a pearl.

The car
Jason had just bought a vintage convertible Mercedes, which he loved, so he sent a toy one down to be photographed in its place.

The tetley tea man
Nobody knew who this belonged to, but they wanted to leave it in because they all loved tea so much!

The mirror
It's actually a picture of the boys with objects reflected in the mirror and if you look very closely you can just make out a Port Vale mascot. Wonder whose idea that was?!

The Buddha
Jason got this on his first trip to Japan and it's very important to him because he fell in love with the country.

The letter blocks
If you were to take all of them out of the picture, they would spell – you guessed it – Take That.

The bracelet

(Plastic coloured stars to the left of the clown with a T block in the middle). This belonged to Adam Ant. He went into the studio while they were doing the cover shoot and when he heard it was for Take That, he said, 'Great! I'm a fan!' and gave them his bracelet. The boys were very impressed!

The clowns

There are five in there in all, and each one is meant to represent a different member of the band.

As the band geared up for the 1995 Nobody Else Tour, there was trouble in the ranks…

Robbie had become unhappy with everything that Take That's wholesome boy-next-door appeal represented. And he was unhappy with the recent attempts to establish a new, raunchier image that he thought was too obviously stage-managed to be taken seriously.

He had become sick and tired of his role as a teenage heart-throb and had actually started to look mildly embarrassed by the whole Take That scene. As a result, he started to play-up even more than usual on tour and during TV performances. He was forever sticking his tongue out or pulling silly faces, anything rather than pretend to look sexy or cute or whatever was the order of that particular day.

Robbie started going to more parties, staying out longer, partying harder. He was going in a completely different direction to the other four members of the group.

The rules

Even at this late stage in their careers, when the five members of the band were kings of the pop world, they were still ruled by Nigel Martin-Smith. Nigel's original terms still applied… they had to look smart (no beards); they must act in a friendly and enthusiastic manner at all times; they must always be accompanied by a minder in public; drinking or drug taking was out, as was asking for more than two weeks off a year. They weren't allowed to copy anybody else's style, or name-check the competition. And they still weren't allowed girlfriends!

Insiders at the time said that money was another reason for Robbie's unhappiness. Even though Take That were one of the decade's most successful pop groups, Robbie felt that he could earn even more as a solo artist. There were even rumours of an interest in Hollywood roles.

End of the road for Robbie

Robbie wanted to be taken seriously and more importantly he felt that he was now old enough to start living his own life. 'I'm doing my job, I'm doing everything that is asked of me, and I'm doing it well,' he said. 'And at the same time I'm going out.' Which, of course, wasn't in the rules.

Glastonbury

But the catalyst to Robbie leaving Take That was his trip to Glastonbury in June 1995. While the whole world was shocked to see pictures of Rob with bleached blond hair and a blacked-out front tooth hanging out with rock's bad boys, the rest of his band was appalled...

He had long wanted to be taken seriously as a musician and he saw this as the first step to his new life... 'I was a bit apprehensive at first,' he admitted later, 'because you read all this stuff about Noel and Liam and the lads and I was wondering how they were going to take to me. But it was top. I walked in and Liam goes, "Take f****** what?" And that was it. I knew we'd have a laugh.'

Rob was plastered all over the papers with one arm round Liam Gallagher, the other clutching a cigarette and his eyes looking decidedly unfocussed. It was obviously no tea party. His behaviour that weekend raised more than a few eyebrows especially as he was going round signing autographs as 'Robbie Williams, nutter'.

When he arrived back in London and met up with the rest of Take That, he was still on a high. Apparently Robbie said that Glastonbury was top! He told them that he had hung out with Jarvis of Pulp and the boys from Oasis. Robbie's mood was not contagious and his reception was rather frosty to say the least. All he was greeted with were muffled mumblings of 'Really?', 'Oh.' and 'Let's rehearse.' Shortly afterwards a band meeting was called to discuss his behaviour. Again.

Rob was plastered all over the papers with one arm round Liam Gallagher, the other clutching a fag and his eyes looking decidedly unfocussed...

And then there were four

ROBBIE

On July 14, 1995 Robbie left the band. The headlines in all the newspapers read 'I quit!' Thousands of fans were left stunned. Take That were only weeks away from a tour, and Robbie wasn't going to be part of it.

Take That were rehearsing for their forthcoming mega-spectacular stage show in a studio in Stockport when Robbie was called to a band meeting just after lunch.

The band was worried about the tour as Robbie didn't seem to be giving a 100% at rehearsals. Everyone felt he was making it clear by his behaviour, that he didn't want to be part of the Take That anymore. One of the show's routines had Robbie throwing Jason backwards and they were worried that if Robbie wasn't up to it, Jason could break his neck. So they sat him down and asked him if he wanted to do the shows or not. Mark said later that they had seen that Robbie was unhappy and that they didn't want to put him through the tour. Rumours abound about what really happened in those last few days, but what is certain is that eventually Robbie walked.

…what is certain is that Robbie walked.

Robbie has recalled walking across the room to the door, looking back at the band and realizing that it was over. Take That folklore has it that he walked out, waited a couple of seconds, walked back in laughing and then left for the last time.

Robbie has never seen any of the band again, except for Mark.

Never forget

Whenever Gary played the band a demo of a new song, he would put it on and say, 'Right...' But when it came to *Never forget*, he put it on and said, 'Pay attention to the lyrics...'

Gary went up to Howard and said, 'Listen, Doug, this is one for you.' And that was how Howard came to be lead vocalist of the last ever, original Take That song.

Jason said that the lyrics of the song blew him away, especially as Gary usually wrote about love and relationships. Gary was also delighted with the lyrics. They spoke of their pasts and were very simple in their sentiment. Through the words he aired their feelings about where they had been and where they had got to, of what they had been and what they had become. The poignancy of the words was undeniably powerful.

The band all loved the single sleeve for *Never forget* as it cleverly showed them all as young boys holding a poster of how they looked at the time the song was recorded.

Never forget
Released July 1995
Highest chart position 1

Howard was nervous about singing lead on such a big track. It was a hard song to sing, and it took a very long time for him to record. When they played the demo through everyone thought his vocal on the track was amazing.

Jason said that he'd never had any doubt in Howard's vocal ability and that despite his lack of confidence he had a superb ear for music. Howard never went out of tune and he could pick harmonies out of nowhere. All the band members were thrilled for Howie to finally come to the front and shine.

Jason said that the lyrics of the song blew him away, especially as Gary usually wrote about love and relationships.

Mark actually helped put together the compilation video for the track. 'We wanted to try and get across what had happened to us in Take That. I remember I travelled down to London with about twelve videos under my arm taken from our camcorders and some poor sod had to sieve through it all for the best shots.'

Although universally loved by the band, there was another side to this track for them as Mark pointed out at the time. 'There will always be a bit of sadness with this song. It was written about five of us and now there are only four. But the show must go on.'

How deep is your love

A COVER V

After *Never forget*, the boys had decided to do a cover version as their next single. It was Howard who suggested the Bee Gees track, *How deep is your love* as he'd always remembered it from the *Saturday Night Fever* soundtrack. They had actually done a demo of it a few years before, but hadn't thought it quite worked at the time. The band decided that they didn't want to do a typical romantic video of them strolling through the countryside with a pretty girl each, so they came up with a much darker scenario – a cross between *Misery* and *Silence of the Lambs*.

RSION

How deep is your love
Released February 1996
Highest chart position 1

Paula Hamilton, who was a top model at the time, played the crazed woman who kidnapped them all. The band were told that they were going to be tied up, put in a van and driven to a cliff top, where one of them was going to be pushed over, but they weren't told who it was going to be. Gary said at the time, 'As soon as I heard that I thought I bet I'm going to draw the short straw – I usually do.' He was right.

Howard doesn't have the fondest memories of the video shoot. He said that they were tied up in chairs for hours, and couldn't get out – it took too long to take all the gaffer tape off. He said he had a chair taped to his bottom for ten hours!

They came up with a much darker scenario for the video – a cross between *Misery* and *Silence of the Lambs*.

Take That take a bow

On Tuesday, February 13, 1996 at 1pm, incidentally Robbie's 22nd birthday, Take That called a press conference at the Hilton Hotel in Manchester and announced that they were going to split up.

It was left to Gary to break the news...

He confirmed that the rumours were true, and *How deep is your love* would be Take That's last single together. After the single, he told the assembled members of the press, they would release a *Greatest Hits* album. He stressed, just to be clear for the somewhat stunned journalists, that from here on in, there would be no more Take That.

For once the press were speechless. While everyone had speculated about what was going to be said at the conference that was called just 24 hours previously – was Robbie re-joining the band? Were they going to squash the rumours they were to split? No one was quite prepared for it to be all over...

Silence reigned in the room, so it was left to Mark to get the ball rolling. He asked if anyone had any questions.

No one was quite prepared for it to be all over.....

The press wanted to know whether the decision to split had been mutual or had come from individual members of the band.

Mark responded to the question saying that after their Christmas break they had all come to the same conclusion independently – there was no individual instigator.

The end

Naturally the press wanted to know how the boys felt about the possibility of each of them falling out of the public eye – disappearing without a trace. Their response was typically candid. Mark admitted that it would probably be easier for Gary as he was already a respected songwriter. For the other three, he conceded that obscurity might beckon!

When the band split up The Samaritans set up telephone help lines to counsel distraught fans.

The boys admitted that they were apprehensive about the future but that they saw it as a new beginning, something to be relished and not afraid of. Jason wanted to stress that this was a positive thing for each of them to branch out as individuals. Jason, always the sensitive one and a deep thinker, would have been worried about any negativity affecting each of them on their new paths.

Howard wanted to stress that the boys were still friends and would remain so. He somewhat idealistically stated that they would still see each other after the split. It is sad to reflect on this, as we know with hindsight, that those moments of continuing to hang out together didn't actually often happen.

Towards the end of the press conference, Jason offered a ray of hope to fans. He said that for the time being they had taken Take That as far as they could, but he didn't rule out them doing a comeback one day! The fans probably didn't expect to have to wait quite as long as they did for Take That to make their next move.

The press conference lasted for about 45 minutes. The boys thanked everyone for coming and for all their support over the years. They were then herded out for photos with the 40 or so waiting photographers before being driven away, separately, through the hordes of screaming and wailing girls outside.

But that wasn't the absolute end right there, less than a week later, Take That honoured their commitments and performed together for one last time at that year's Brit Awards where they also picked up the Best Single Award for *Back for good*.

The end.
Or is it the beginning?

Their greatest hits

Live

One of Mark's favourite live moments was when he performed *Babe* for the very first time. It was in Bournemouth and he was very emotional. 'I was filling up inside. The crowd pretty much sang the song for me – it was beautiful.'

Gary says that he always liked the ballads best live as it meant he didn't have to do too much dancing! A particular favourite was *Babe*, which of course Mark sang, 'I'm literally doing nothing... so that's probably my favourite!'

Babe and *Back for good* were Jason's favourites as he got to show off his guitar skills.

Rather unsurprisingly, Howard's best live performance was *Never forget*, but not just because he sang it, but because of the crowd's reaction. 'The biggest buzz I've ever had on stage.'

Songs

One of Howard's all-time favourite Take That songs was *Back for good* as not only was it a classic track, but it also crossed over to a wider audience and brought them more worldwide success.

It was a more simple choice for Jason... '*Pray*: superb song, brilliant routine, great video.'

Gary has more nostalgic reasons for his choice, *Never forget*. '...because it's just about us...'

Videos

Mark's favourite video was *Never forget* because of all the backstage footage of the band – plus he helped to direct it. He also likes *Babe* because it's like a mini-movie.

Why can't I wake up with you holds fond memories for Howard of the time they all spent together filming it in the chateau in France.

Jason likes *It only takes a minute* because at the time, making videos was still a new experience for them and they were still so excited by everything.

Memories

Howard says that now whenever he sees one of their old videos on TV it always takes him straight back to that time and brings back such fond memories…

Mark is still surprised by what happened to him during his Take That days. He said that he saw himself as being a back-seater in the band, but he probably had been on more covers than any of the others. He said he even got sick of seeing his own face on television or in magazines!

One of Robbie's highlights of his years in Take That was when the band performed their Beatles medley at the Brits. Not only did he have great fun doing it, but he was overwhelmed by the amount of people – and not just your average punters but big celebrities too – who came up to him afterwards to tell him how much they enjoyed it. He felt like a real star.

Robbie goes off the rails

Straight after he left the band, Robbie disappeared. He fled the country and went to stay at George Michael's house in the south of France for a few weeks. He needed to get away from the British press and try to figure out what he was going to do next. After all, Robbie was only 21 when he left Take That, an age when most people haven't made much headway with their careers – Robbie had already been a mega pop star – what could he do next to match the highs that he had had with the band?

On his return to England, he still needed somewhere else to hide out as the nation's press were hounding him. So he hired himself a new manager, Kevin Kinsella, and he went to stay with him and his wife Norma in their house in Cheshire. But unfortunately the relationship didn't work out and six months later Robbie left. Next he moved in with his first serious girlfriend, make-up artist Jacqui Hamilton-Smith.

But by now Robbie was partying big time. He was hanging out at *Browns* nightclub in London with Oasis and in St Tropez with George Michael, Bono, Paula Yates and Michael Hutchence. His behaviour wasn't conducive to a successful relationship and finally Jacqui told him it was over.

As well as living a 24/7 party life, Robbie had also been in legal battles with BMG, the label he was signed to with Take That. He finally became free of them on June 27, 1996 and he signed a deal with Chrysalis Records. Robbie's solo career could finally begin.

…he signed a deal with Chrysalis Records. Robbie's solo career could finally begin.

Robbie got more and more out of control until Elton John literally kidnapped him – according to Robbie – and packed him off to Clouds House Drink and Drugs Rehabilitation Clinic in Salisbury, Wiltshire. It worked. He lost weight and cleaned up his act.

Robbie released his first solo single, a cover of George Michael's *Freedom* in July 1996 – it reached No. 2 in the charts. By now, Take That had split up and Robbie went head-to-head with his old band mate, Gary in April 1997. Robbie's second single, *Old before I die* was beaten to No. 1 by Gary Barlow's *Love won't wait*.

But his career was still going nowhere. His third single, *Lazy days* released in July 1997 only made it to No. 8. This was followed by *South of the border*, which again didn't do very well, charting at 14. Things were not looking good for Robbie Williams.

December 1997 was the real beginning for Robbie when he released *Angels* as his Christmas single. His record company were just about to drop him and this was his last bite at the cherry. Bizarrely, *Angels* was never meant to be a single, just a pleasant album track. Who could ever have foretold the impact this one record was going to have on the music world and, more importantly on Robbie Williams' life?

His first album, *Life thru a lens* stormed back into the charts and his phenomenally successful writing relationship with former Lemon Trees member, Guy Chambers, went on to spawn many more successful and lucrative hits. The second album, *I've been expecting you* produced his first solo number one, *Millennium* in September 1998.

Sing when you're winning was his third album and with such classic moments as the *Rock DJ* video seeing Robbie stripping down to his bare bones, a sell-out tour soon followed.

By 2001 it was almost acceptable to be a Robbie Williams fan and again he did something new. Robbie performed a sell-out show at London's Royal Albert Hall reviving all the old Rat Pack favourites from *Frank Sinatra, Sammy Davis Jr.* and *Dean Martin*. These were later released on the cheekily titled, *Swing when you're winning* album.

Robbie took a year off and bought himself a nice little mansion in the Hollywood Hills where he finally got some respite from the British media. *Escapology* was his fifth solo album and went straight to number one all over Europe.

In 2003, Robbie released the live DVD, *What we did last summer* which became the fastest selling live DVD of all-time. And in June 2003 he performed to over 1.24 million people, rounding off with a record-breaking three consecutive dates at Knebworth playing to another 375,000 people. A live CD was later released.

His record company were just about to drop him…

Shortly afterwards the controversial biography *Feel* was published probing his love life, career and relationships with family and friends. It was a surprise to everyone how someone who has so much could be so lonely.

In October 2004, EMI, who had re-signed Robbie for a staggering £80 million, released a *Greatest Hits* album which went to number one all across Europe.

In February 2006, Robbie fulfilled a life-long ambition by buying a substantial stake in Port Vale Football Club.

It all started out so well for Gary Barlow... After the split there were mumblings about him being the next George Michael and with his first single, *Forever love* beating Robbie Williams to number one, things were looking good.

Gary's second single, *Love won't wait* also topped the charts and his first album, *Open road* sold over a million copies. But it wasn't enough.

He was dumped by RCA, the record company he'd been with since his Take That days.

When Gary's second album, *Stronger* failed to reach the Top 30, he was dumped by RCA, the record company he'd been with since his Take That days.

Gary decided to take a break and his next foray into show business came when he played a hitchhiker in the ITV series, *Heartbeat*.

After piling on the pounds, Gary accepted that his pop star days were probably over and started writing songs for other people. He set up a music company called True North with writer/producer Elliott Kennedy – who wrote many of the Spice Girls hits – and they now write songs for the likes of Blue and Charlotte Church.

Gary is happily married to Dawn, a dancer he first met during a video shoot when he was 17. They bumped into each other briefly over the years, but it was when Dawn was hired by Jason Orange to be a dancer on their very last tour, that things really clicked. The two were married at Gary's Cheshire home in 2000 with Howard as best man. They now have two children, Daniel, five and Emily, three.

Gary accepted that his pop star days were probably over and started writing songs for other people.

What JASON did next

By the time the band split Jason had had enough of show business, so he grabbed his backpack and his guitar and headed off to travel the world with a friend for a year. He spent most of it in India, sitting staring at mountains and the sea contemplating what he was going to do with the rest of his life.

...he grabbed his back-pack and his guitar...

When he returned to the UK, Jason decided to try his hand at acting and enrolled in some drama classes.

His first major role was a part in the Channel 4 Lynda La Plante drama, *Killer Net*, in which he played the sinister and crooked drug-dealing DJ, Brent Moyer.

In 1999 he went on to appear on stage in the comedy *Gob* – about a drug addict poet – at the *King's Head Theatre* in Islington. He earned just £120 a week, but the show won critical acclaim.

He decided to enrol at college and studied psychology and sociology.

But for Jason, even this was too much like being back in the limelight again, so he decided to enrol at college and to study psychology and sociology. Jason is now at his happiest when he's using his brain – quenching his thirst for knowledge. He feels that he's making up for lost time, having never studied at school.

Jason has also dabbled in property developing, but other than that he says that he just really has hobbies. All the members of Take That, apart from Gary Barlow, are said to have walked away with about £4 million each when they split – so with wise investment, they should never have to work again.

Jason is still single although he was linked to a few semi-famous women; page three model Kathy Lloyd, TV presenter Jenny Powell and, of course, Lulu.

Mark was the first member of Take That to release a record after the split and he didn't do too badly. His first two singles, *Child* and *Clementine* both got to number 3 in the charts and his album, *Green man* sold a million copies. But after the success of Take That it was seen as something of a flop and RCA dropped him.

For the next few years he lived a reclusive life in his six-bedroomed house in the Lake District with his girlfriend of 10 years, Joanne. But the relationship failed and the pair split up, although remain good friends to this day.

Mark never gave up songwriting and recording, but after trying numerous times to get a record deal he accepted that it was probably never going to happen and was content to make music for himself. That was until *Celebrity Big Brother*.

For the next few years he lived a reclusive life in his six-bedroomed house in the Lake District.

When he was first offered a place on the show, he thought about turning it down, but he then decided that he'd hidden himself away for too long.

Mark became the unexpected hit of the series, dragging old Take That fans out of hiding and gaining new ones along the way. And amazingly he won! Shortly afterwards he signed a new contract with Island Records and had a Top 5 hit with *Four minute warning*. Unfortunately, his album, *In your own time* totally flopped and he was dropped.

Mark became the unexpected hit of the series, dragging old Take That fans out of hiding and gaining new ones along the way.

The one great thing to come from his exposure on Big Brother was that he got a call from his old band mate Robbie, who invited him to sing on stage with him live at Knebworth.

It seems that the demise of Take That hit Howard the hardest at the time. He has recently admitted that after the announcement was made, he was staying in a London hotel and he went for a walk along the Thames. As he was sitting on the wall he actually thought about throwing himself in the river. Obviously he didn't.

Howard spent his first year after Take That split lying in bed watching Richard and Judy.

Howard spent his first year after Take That split lying in bed watching Richard and Judy on *This Morning* every day. He was caught up in a legal row over royalties with RCA, which meant that he couldn't release any of the 100-or-so songs he had written. He got so bored that he took up golf and even learnt how to garden. But all he really wanted was to release the album he had, (and still has ready to go). Howard had talks with a few record labels, but no one was willing to give the ex-Take Thatter a go.

Howard has always continued songwriting, he wrote the theme tune for Channel 4's now defunct *Planet Pop* programme and even had a hit when '90s pop star Kavana released one of his tracks. But it is as an international dance DJ that Howard has really made his name.

Under the name, DJ HD, Howard is now a highly paid and highly sought after DJ, playing the top clubs of Europe and regularly headlining in dance mecca, Ibiza.

Howard has two children, is single and lives in Southampton.

Under the name, DJ HD, Howard is now a highly paid and highly sought after DJ.

The Fans

They have screamed with joy, wailed with despondency and waited patiently for the day when the boys would get back together.

Take That tour secrets

- The boys all used to have a vitamin B injection at the start of each tour which helped to ward off any illnesses and gave them a bit of extra energy. It would last for about a month.

- On the Take That and Party tour, their tour bus only had four beds so each night they'd fight over who got to sleep in them.

- They used to drink honey and lemon every day to help their voices and ward off colds.

- They were always getting told off for shouting too much on stage by the musical director in case it damaged their voices.

- Max Beasley, star of *Bodies* and *Hotel Babylon* was the percussionist on a couple of tours and still remains a close friend to the band – particularly Robbie – to this day.

- They used to get most nervous playing Manchester NEC as all their friends and family were there.

- An hour before they went on stage they had a rule that **nobody** could come into the dressing room.

- Their nightly ritual before going on stage was to all hug each other and say, 'Have a good one!'

- While on tour Gary used to have Golden Grahams and white toast with marmalade for breakfast every day.

- Robbie often used to end up sleeping in Mark's room in hotels as he used to get scared on his own.

Reunion

It was one of the most talked about TV documentaries of the year – *Take That… For the record*. Shown on Wednesday, November 16, 2005 on ITV1, it was the first time for 10 years that, hopefully, all of Take That would be reunited to talk candidly about their time in the band and everything that had happened to them since. A nation of ex-Take Thatters sat glued…

The band revealed that on the day they finally split, they each got into separate cars and went their own ways. Mark said it was like hearses taking them to their own funerals. None of them then saw each other for three years.

None of them then saw each other for three years.

It was inconceivable to most that these shiny bright-eyed boys of pop, who had lived in each others' pockets for seven years and who we all thought were the best of friends, should just drift away from each other. Gary now admits that he thinks they handled the break-up all wrong. But it turned out that there has been some contact – Gary worked on one of Mark's solo albums and Gary and Howard used to occasionally meet up because they both had young children. But that was it. They hadn't all been in a room together until the documentary and they most definitely hadn't talked about the Take That years.

The most enduring memory of the TV show, was when the four final members arrived individually at Cliveden House, a luxury hotel in Berkshire. They gathered in the lounge and while conversation was stilted at first, gradually they relaxed as one would say… 'Do you remember the time…' and they'd be off on a happy trail of reminiscing about the heady days when they were the kings of pop. It just seemed a shame that it had taken them 10 years to be able to get to the point where they could look back fondly, instead of through a mist of anger and bitterness.

Reunion

But the tableau wasn't quite complete. They were still missing one vital part of their pop history, Robbie Williams. Robbie had taken part in the programme and had even appeared to have let some of his resentment go, but no one knew whether he was going to turn up at Cliveden or not. It was excruciating to watch the four of them sitting there on the edge of the seats, nervously twitching every time a car pulled up, or a door opened.

> Robbie stayed away. Perhaps too much had been said by him.

But Robbie stayed away from the reunion. Perhaps too much had been said by him, ranting about the bullying he had suffered at the hands of the others – whatever the reason, he was a no show. He did, however, send a video message to the rest of the band... He spoke to the four individually and apologized for some of the things he had said in the past, he even suggested that he would like to meet up with them again someday – well with Howard, Jason and Mark at least. To Gary, all he admitted was that he was an amazing songwriter. It seemed that there were some things that could just not be forgotten, or forgiven. Although, rather tellingly, Robbie then went on to say that he envied Gary his quiet, stable family life. He even said he would swap everything that he had for what Gary's got. But knowing Robbie, his tongue could well have been planted firmly in his cheek. Who can tell?

Two days before the programme was shown, there was a premiere for the press and a party afterwards which the final four members attended. They admitted that they were absolutely terrified about the sort of response they would get. Would anyone still care? You can imagine their faces when they turned up, not only to a sea of cameras flashing, but also to hordes of screaming girls – albeit slightly older than your average boy band fan. One thing is true. People definitely do still care...

Future

After being put on crash diets, told to give up the drink and fags and holed up in a dance studio in Chiswick for three months, the boys were finally off on their comeback tour. The tour that they were nervous about doing – in case no one turned up – and which, in fact, sold out in 30 minutes flat. Five times quicker than their old mate Robbie Williams!

In fact, so intense was the demand for tickets, that Wembley Arena's website crashed and tickets were being sold on Ebay for hundreds of pounds!

JASON ORANGE   GARY BARLOW

After the allegedly amicable parting of ways of the band and Nigel Martin-Smith shortly after the tour was announced, rumours abounded that there could possibly be a surprise guest appearance of a certain Mr Robert Peter Williams at one of the shows... Of course we won't know the outcome of that until the tour has finished. But fingers crossed!

There are more rumours about after tour plans, including an album of new material. The boys have been back in the studio working on fresh ideas – plus of course a few never-seen-before gems that Gary has up his sleeve – and every indication is that there will be a brand new album out later this year...

The future of Take That has never been brighter!

MARK OWEN

HOWARD DONALD

Discography

Do what you like
July 1991
Highest chart position 82

Promises
November 1991
Highest chart position 38

Once you've tasted love
January 1992
Highest chart position 47

It only takes a minute
May 1992
Highest chart position 7

I found heaven
August 1992
Highest chart position 15

A million love songs
September 1992
Highest chart position 7

Could it be magic
December 1992
Highest chart position 3

Why can't I wake up with you
February 1993
Highest chart position 2

Pray
July 1993
Highest chart position 1

Relight my fire
September 1993
Highest chart position 1

Babe
December 1993
Highest chart position 1

Everything changes
March 1994
Highest chart position 1

Love ain't here anymore
June 1994
Highest chart position 3

Sure
October 1994
Highest chart position 1

Back for good
March 1995
Highest chart position 1

Never forget
July 1995
Highest chart position 1

How deep is your love
February 1996
Highest chart position 1

Take That and party
August 1992
Highest chart position 2

Everything changes
October 1993
Highest chart position 1

Nobody else
May 1995
Highest chart position 1

Greatest hits
May 1996
Highest chart position 1

Never forget – greatest hits
November 2005
Highest chart position 2

ACKNOWLEDGMENTS

The publishers would like to thank the following for their kind permission to reproduce their photographs:
r = right; l = left; a = above; b = below; c = centre; t = top.

Cover: Bernhard Kuhmstead/Retna; Page 7: Bernhard Kuhmstead/Retna; Page 12: Empics; Page 13: Retna; Page 14cl: Collections; Page14cr: Rex Features; Page 15: Rex Features; Page 16cl: Rex Features; Page 16cr: Collections; Page 17: Rex Features; Page 18cl: Rex Features; Page 18br: Rex Features; Page 19: Rex Features; Page 20cl: Rex Features; Page 20cr: Collections; Page 21:Rex Features; Page 22: Rex Features; Page 23: Rex Features; Page 24: Rex Features; Page 25: Retna; Page 26:cr: Rex Features; Page 26bl: Rex Features; Page 27: Rex Features; Page 28: Rex Features; Page 29: Rex Features; Page 30: MEN Syndication; Page 31: LFI; Page 32: Rex Features; Page 33: Rex Features; Page 34: Retna: Page 35: Rex Features; Page 36: Retna: Page 37: Rex Features; Page 38c: Retna; Page 38b: Rex Features; Page 39: Retna; Page 40: Rex Features; Page 41: Rex Features; Page 42: Rex Features: Page 43: Rex Features; Page 44: Rex Features; Page 45: Redferns; Page 46: Rex Features; Page 47: Retna: Page 48: Rex Features: Page 49: Rex Features; Page 50: Rex Features: Page 51: Rex Features; Page 52: Rex Features; Page 53: Rex Features; Page 54: Rex Features; Page 55: Rex Features; Page 56: Retna; Page 57: Rex Features; Page 58: Rex Features; Page 59: Retna; Page 60c: Rex Features; Page 60b: Rex Features; Page 61: Rex Features; Page 63: Rex Features; Page 64: Empics; Page 65: Rex Features; Page 66: Alpha; Page 67: Alpha; Page 68: Redferns; Page 69: Rex Features; Page 70: MEN Syndication; Page 71: Alpha; Page 72: MEN Syndication; Page 73: Retna; Page 77: Retna; Page 78: Rex Features; Page 79: Rex Features; Page 80: Rex Features; Page 81: bigpicturephoto. com; Page 83: Rex Features; Page 84: Rex Features; Page 85: Rex Features: Page 86: Rex Features; Page 87: Rex Features; Page 88: Rex Features; Page 89: Rex Features; Page 90: Retna; Page 91: Retna; Page 92: Rex Features; Page 93: bigpicturephoto.com; Page 94: Rex Features; Page 95: Redferns: Page 96: Rex Features; Page 97: Rex Features; Page 98: Rex Features; Page 99: Rex Features; Page 100: Rex Features; Page 101: Rex Features; Page 102: Rex Features; Page 103: Rex Features; Page 104l: Redferns; Page 104r (from top to bottom): Rex Features; bigpicturephoto.com; Rex Features; Rex Features; Page 105a: Rex Features; Page 105b: Rex Features; Page 106: LFI; Page 107: Empics; Page 108: Rex Features; Page 109a: Rex Features; Page 109b: Rex Features; Page 110: Rex Features; Page 111a: Rex Features; Page 111b: Rex Features; Pages 112/113: Rex Features